Have You Seen the Yellow Wattle Flowers?

By Mary Ozies

Library For All Ltd.

Library For All is an Australian not for profit organisation with a mission to make knowledge accessible to all via an innovative digital library solution. Visit us at libraryforall.org

Have You Seen the Yellow Wattle Flowers?

First published 2023

Published by Library For All Ltd
Email: info@libraryforall.org
URL: libraryforall.org

Our Yarning logo design by Jason Lee, Bidjipidji Art

Original illustrations by keishart

Have You Seen the Yellow Wattle Flowers?
Ozies, Mary
ISBN: 978-1-923110-40-3
SKU03382

Have You Seen the Yellow Wattle Flowers?

Mook Mook saw bright yellow flowers suddenly appear in the bush near his home.

Mook Mook wanted to know more about the yellow flowers.

He asked his grandma, Mimi, where they came from.

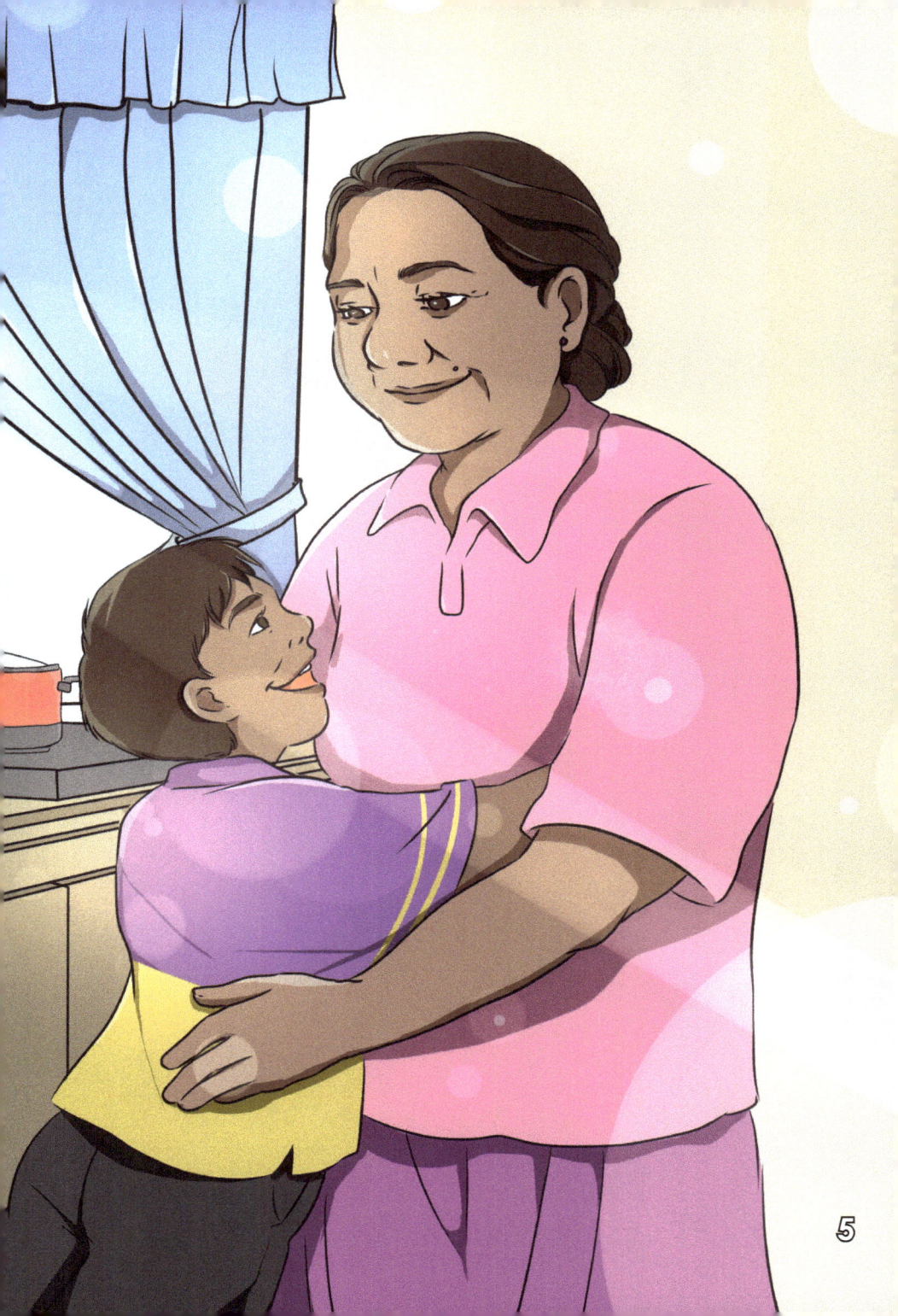

Mimi told Mook Mook the yellow flowers came to tell us about the bush and sea life.

The yellow flowers tell us the stingrays swimming in the sea are fat and ready to catch.

The yellow flowers tell
us the fish living on
the sea reef are fat and
ready to eat, too.

The yellow flowers tell us the big boab nuts on the tree in the bush are ripe and ready to crack and eat.

The yellow flowers tell us the magabala on the vines are ripe and ready to pick and eat, too.

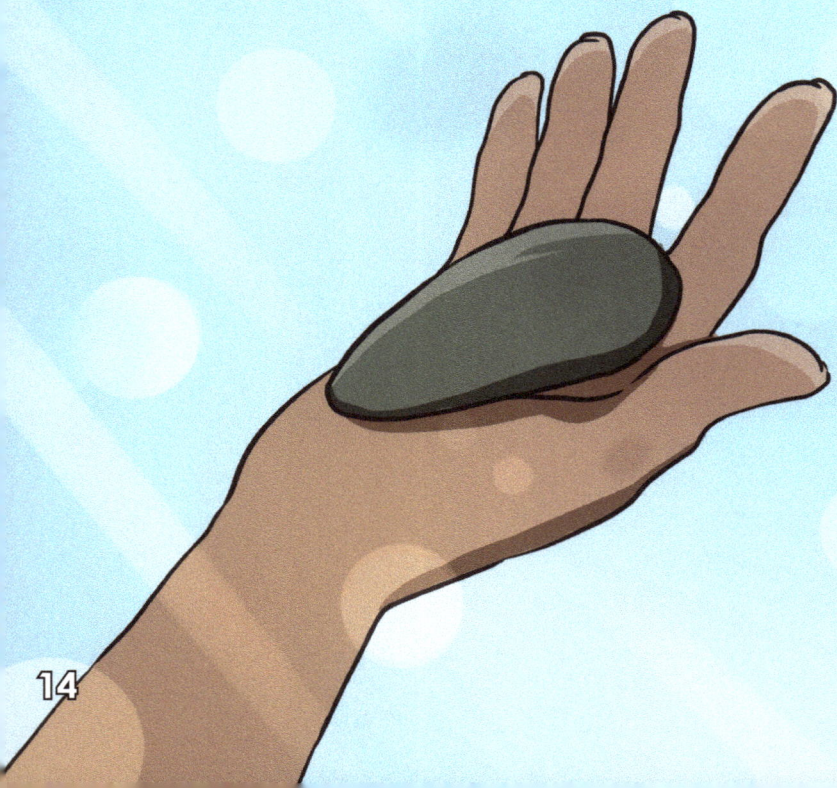

Soon, all the yellow flowers
in the bush were gone and
that made Mook Mook sad.

Mimi told Mook Mook not to feel sad, because the yellow flowers will come to visit again next year.

This made Mook Mook happy.

You can use these questions to talk about this book with your family, friends and teachers.

What did you learn from this book?

Describe this book in one word. Funny? Scary? Colourful? Interesting?

How did this book make you feel when you finished reading it?

What was your favourite part of this book?

download our reader app
getlibraryforall.org

About the author

Mary is a Djugun Elder living in Broome, Western Australia. She grew up in Derby, Western Australia, with cultural ties to both Nyikina and Djugun language groups. Mary learnt about seasonal food sources from her ancestors by oral history while hunting and gathering with her family.

The story of *Have You Seen the Yellow Wattle Flowers* is a story about Birramingl Time. The cool, dry season in the northwest tells when it is the best time to catch and collect certain traditional tucker from the sea and bush. The character of Mook Mook is the imaginary friend of Mary's youngest son who loved to learn about his natural environment.

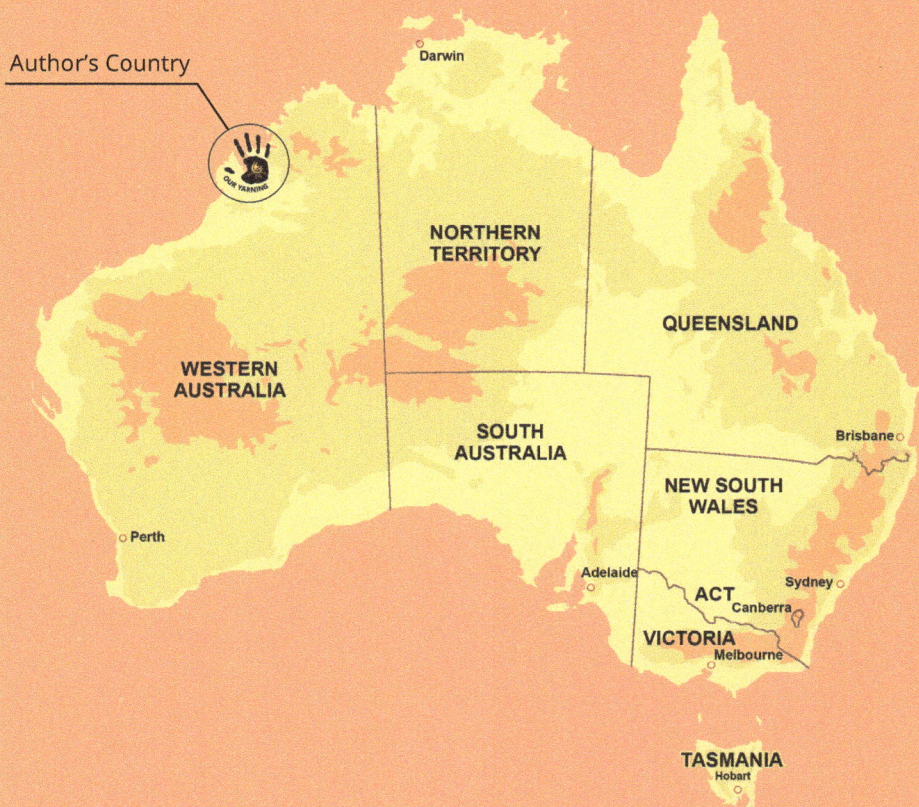

Author's Country

Darwin

NORTHERN
TERRITORY

QUEENSLAND

WESTERN
AUSTRALIA

SOUTH
AUSTRALIA

Brisbane

NEW SOUTH
WALES

Perth

Adelaide

ACT
Canberra

Sydney

VICTORIA

Melbourne

TASMANIA
Hobart

Our Yarning

Want to discover more books from this collection? Our Yarning is a collection of books written by Aboriginal and Torres Strait Islander peoples across Australia.

We know that children learn better, and enjoy reading more, when they see themselves in the stories, characters and illustrations of the books they read.

To download the app, visit the Google Play Store on any Android device and search 'Our Yarning'.

libraryforall.org

www.ingramcontent.com/pod-product-compliance
Lightning Source LLC
Chambersburg PA
CBHW042347040426
42448CB00019B/3434